CCSS **Genre** Expository Text

Essential Question
How do landmarks help us
understand our country's story?

W9-BEZ-669

The
National Mall

by Elizabeth Brereton

Introduction

The National Mall is in the center of Washington, D.C. The **White House** looks out over the Mall. So does the United States **Capitol**.

The National Mall is an important gathering place in our nation's capital. People come to the Mall to see a new president be sworn in. On the Fourth of July, people can watch fireworks at the Mall.

The United States Capitol is at the top of the Mall.

The National Mall is home to many important buildings, such as **memorials** and museums. People can learn about American history there.

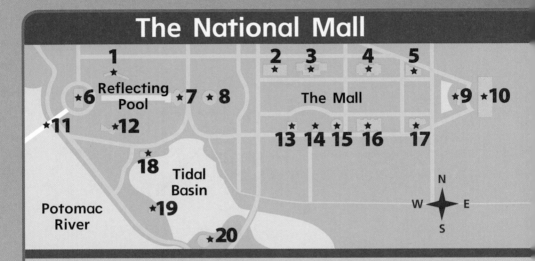

The National Mall

1

★

★6 Reflecting ★7 ★8
       Pool

★11   ★12

2 3   4 5
★ ★   ★ ★

The Mall

★9 ★10

★ ★ ★ ★   ★
13 14 15 16 17

18
★

Tidal
Basin

Potomac   ★19
River

★20

N
W ─┼─ E
S

KEY

1. Vietnam Veterans Memorial
2. Museum of American History
3. Museum of Natural History
4, 5. National Gallery of Art
6. Lincoln Memorial
7. World War II Memorial
8. Washington Monument
9. Ulysses S. Grant Memorial
10. The Capitol
11. Arlington Memorial Bridge
12. Korean War Veterans Memorial

13. Freer Gallery
14. Museum of African Art
15. Hirshhorn Museum and Sculpture Garden
16. Air and Space Museum
17. Museum of the American Indian
18. The Martin Luther King, Jr. Memorial
19. FDR Memorial
20. Jefferson Memorial

3

The Washington Monument is at the center of the National Mall. This landmark is named for George Washington. He was America's first president. The **obelisk** is 555.5 feet high. It is the tallest structure in Washington, D.C.

By law, nothing in Washington is allowed to be taller than the Washington Monument.

Uyen Le/Photodisc/Getty Images

There are other monuments to presidents, too. The Lincoln Memorial honors Abraham Lincoln. He was the president during the Civil War and ended slavery in the United States.

IN THIS TEMPLE
AS IN THE HEARTS OF THE PEOPLE
FOR WHOM HE SAVED THE UNION
THE MEMORY OF ABRAHAM LINCOLN
IS ENSHRINED FOREVER

This statue of Abraham Lincoln sits in Lincoln Memorial.

The Jefferson Memorial honors our third president. Jefferson also wrote the Declaration of Independence.

The Jefferson Memorial is made of white marble.

The Roosevelt Memorial honors Franklin Delano Roosevelt. He was the president for four terms. He led the United States through World War II.

Roosevelt was President from 1933 to 1945.

Frank Tozier/Alamy

Martin Luther King, Jr. Memorial

Martin Luther King, Jr. worked toward getting equal rights for African Americans. The memorial has a statue of King carved from rock. King was an important figure of hope for many Americans.

Ulysses S. Grant was a general in the American Civil War. He was a skilled military leader. His memorial is three massive **sculptures**. The central one is a statue of Grant riding a horse.

Ulysses Grant became the eighteenth president of the United States.

STOP AND CHECK

Who has been honored on the Mall?

7

Chapter 2

War Memorials

The columns of the World War II Memorial represent the states and territories that made up the United States at the time.

War memorials honor the people who served during wartime. The World War II memorial has columns around a pool. More than 4,000 gold stars decorate a curved wall. Each star represents 100 American soldiers who died in the war.

This statue is part of the Vietnam Veterans Memorial.

The Vietnam War was America's longest war. The Vietnam Veterans Memorial was finished in 1982. This memorial is for the 58,000 Americans who died or went missing during the war. Their names are written on the two walls of the memorial.

Another memorial honors American veterans of the Korean War. There are 19 sculptures of soldiers at the site. About 2,500 images of soldiers from the war appear on a wall.

These sculptures are part of the Korean War Veterans Memorial.

STOP AND CHECK

Why have the war memorials been built?

Chapter 3
Collecting America's History

The Air and Space Museum has early airplanes.

The National Mall has a number of museums. One of them is the Air and Space Museum. Visitors can see the Wright Brothers' first plane. They can also see the suits that the astronauts wore on the moon.

There are traces of transportation history at the Museum of American History, too. There are trains from the 1800s and a 1950s station wagon.

Museums and art galleries give clues about other cultures. The Museum of African Art has African masks, paintings, and crafts. The Freer Gallery is famous for its Asian art.

The National Gallery of Art displays art from all around the world. The Hirshhorn Museum and Sculpture Garden has a collection of sculptures.

The African elephant is a popular exhibit at the Museum of Natural History.

This sculpture is at the Hirshhorn Museum and Sculpture Garden.

UP CLOSE

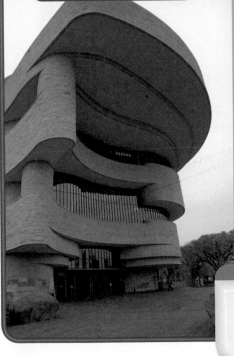

Museum of the American Indian

The National Museum of the American Indian shows Native American culture and history. It has historical items, films, and photos.

STOP AND CHECK

Why are museums important?

Conclusion

Arlington Memorial Bridge is the "foot" of the National Mall. It links the Mall to Arlington Cemetery. That is where many of America's heroes are buried.

The National Mall is a place of which every American can be proud.

Visitors can see the Lincoln Memorial from Arlington Bridge.

John Aikins/CORBIS

Respond to Reading

Summarize

Use details from *The National Mall* to summarize the selection. Your graphic organizer may help.

Main Idea
Detail
Detail
Detail

Text Evidence

1. How do you know that *The National Mall* is an expository text? Genre

2. Why is the National Mall important? Main Idea and Key Details

3. Find the word *pool* on page 8. Use clues to figure out its meaning. Multiple-Meaning Words

4. What is one interesting detail about the National Mall? Write about Reading

Compare Texts
Read about the tallest monument in the United States.

GATEWAY ARCH

Gateway Arch is in St. Louis. It is the tallest monument in the United States. The arch was built to honor the people who explored and settled the West. It also honors President Thomas Jefferson. He wanted the United States to stretch right across North America.

Many people began their journey west from St. Louis.

A grand monument was the idea of Luther Ely Smith. He wanted people to know how much the explorers and settlers had done for America.

A competition was held to choose a design for the arch. An architect named Eero Saarinen won the competition. Building began in 1963. The arch was opened in 1967.

Explorers William Clark (left) and Meriwether Lewis (right) began their journey west in St. Louis.

The Gateway Arch is 630 feet tall. Visitors can ride a tram to the top. The journey takes four minutes. Visitors can see all of St. Louis from the top.

About 900 tons of stainless steel were used in the arch.

Brand X Pictures/PunchStock

Make Connections

Which is your favorite of the monuments mentioned, and why?

Essential Question

How is the Gateway Arch like the other monuments you read about?

Text to Text

Glossary

Capitol *(KA-puh-tuhl)* the place where the nation's laws are made *(page 2)*

memorials *(muh-MAWR-ee-uhlz)* structures that remind people of a person or an event *(page 3)*

obelisk *(O-buh-lisk)* a four-sided pillar that gets narrower as it gets taller and ends in a point *(page 4)*

sculptures *(SKUHLP-churz)* artworks made from hard materials such as stone or wood *(page 7)*

White House *(HWIGHT HOWS)* the place where the President lives *(page 2)*

Index

Focus on
Social Studies

Purpose To find out about a monument

What to Do

Step 1 Choose a monument or memorial you are interested in—not one that you have read about in this book.

Step 2 Find out as much as you can about it—where it is, its size, and interesting features.

Step 3 Make a poster to attract visitors to the monument or memorial. Draw it and label its features.

Conclusion What do you think is the most important role of monuments?